*Looping Letters:*
*I Want to Improve*
*My Handwriting!*

# Looping Letters:

# I Want to Improve

# My Handwriting!

A Handwriting Workbook for **Teenagers**

By Jonell Patricia Murphy

# Looping Letters: I Want to Improve My Handwriting!

## By Jonell Patricia Murphy

Other books by Jonell P. Murphy

Pull

If You Don't Like It Here, There's the Door!

Copyright © 2017 Jonell Patricia Murphy.

All rights reserved. No part of this book may be reproduced, stored, or transmitted by any means—whether auditory, graphic, mechanical, or electronic—without written permission of the author, except in the case of brief excerpts used in critical articles and reviews. Unauthorized reproduction of any part of this work is illegal and is punishable by law.

Hershey's product images in this book are not meant to be an endorsement.

ISBN: 978-1-4834-7432-8 (sc)
ISBN: 978-1-4834-7433-5 (e)

Because of the dynamic nature of the Internet, any web addresses or links contained in this book may have changed since publication and may no longer be valid. The views expressed in this work are solely those of the author and do not necessarily reflect the views of the publisher, and the publisher hereby disclaims any responsibility for them.

Any people depicted in stock imagery provided by Thinkstock are models, and such images are being used for illustrative purposes only.
Certain stock imagery © Thinkstock.

Lulu Publishing Services rev. date: 03/16/2018

To my family that I love: Louise, Robert, Roland, and the late Joseph P. Murphy, Sr.

In loving memory of Joseph Porter Murphy, Jr.

To my friend Teresa Parsons

To my friend and former business partner Naipaul Sookdeo

To: All those that strive to improve in Newark Public Schools. Especially those at Weequahic High School, Malcolm X. Shabazz High School, Brick Peshine, and Hawthorne Avenue School.

To all the Murphy Fisher Brown Family members of Daytona Beach, Florida and beyond.

## Acknowledgements

Thanks to:

Campbell's Soup Company

Hershey's Chocolate and Confectionery Corporation

Wikipedia.org.

Schoolhouse Fonts.com

Fonts4Teachers.com

Lulu Publishing

Rising Tide Capital of Newark and Jersey City

Winston C. Trumpet, my Instructor and author of **Crossing the Mindfield of Your Mind.**

Cynthia Pullen, my RTC Business coach and author of **I'll Still Here: Triumph Over Breast Cancer Through Faith and Holistic Healing.**

I ♡ Hawaii and Alaska that were left off of the United States image on page 43. This workbook was put together by computer and by hand.

Thinkstock.com

Getty Images.com

I will be using two styles of cursive letters in this book. If you see different letters on some pages it's okay.

**D'Nealian cursive**

*A B C D E F G H I J K L M N O P*
*Q R S T U V W X Y Z a b c d e f g*
*h i j k l m n o p q r s t u v*
*w x y z*

**Traditional cursive**

*A B C D E F G H I J K L M N O*
*P Q R S T U V W X Y Z a b c d e*
*f g h I j k l m n o p q r s t u v*
*w x y z*

# Introduction

**Looping Letters: I Want to Improve My Handwriting!** was created to help teenagers learn or improve their ability to write in the cursive hand. And (oops), their ability to read it.

Many school systems around the country have abandon the practice of teaching cursive writing. It was felt that, in an age of computer and digital device dominance, good penmanship is no longer necessary.

But, as a Substitute teacher for twenty years, as I watched thousands of children (although, intelligent enough to master those digital devices) struggle to even print their names on my attendance sheets, I saw firsthand, from school to school, penmanship must be saved.

Jonell P. Murphy

P.S. Please use a pencil so you can erase and practice again and again. Have fun!

## Table of Contents

| | |
|---|---|
| How to slant your paper/ How to hold your pencil | 3 |
| How to start each letter: follow the arrows | 4 |
| Trace and Copy Practice | 11 |
| Upper case letters | |
| Lower case letters | |
| How to Link the letters | 29 |
| Word Practice: Trace, Then Copy | 30 |
| Hardest Ones -- One More Time | 52 |
| School Words | 54 |
| How to tell Time on an Old-Fashioned (analog) Clock | 58 |
| The Pledge of Allegiance   Copy | 68 |
| Part of President John F. Kennedy's speech Write in Cursive | 69 |
| President George W. Bush and George H.W. Bush quotes Copy | 70 |
| President Abraham Lincoln quote Copy | 71 |

For best results, Left-handed people slant their paper to the right.

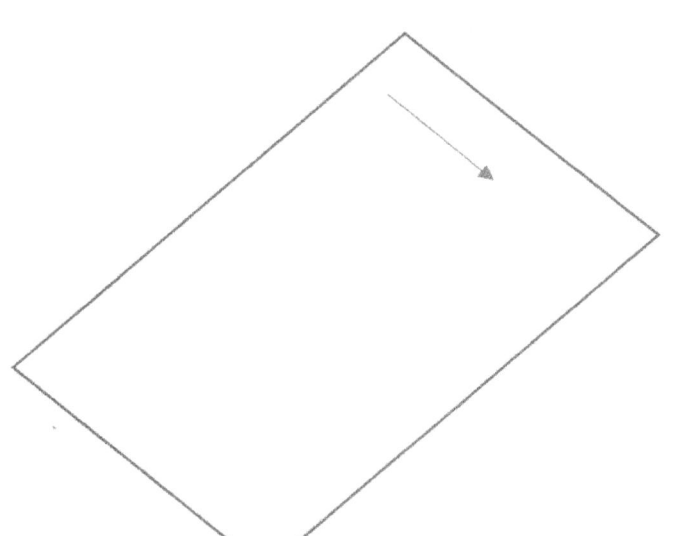

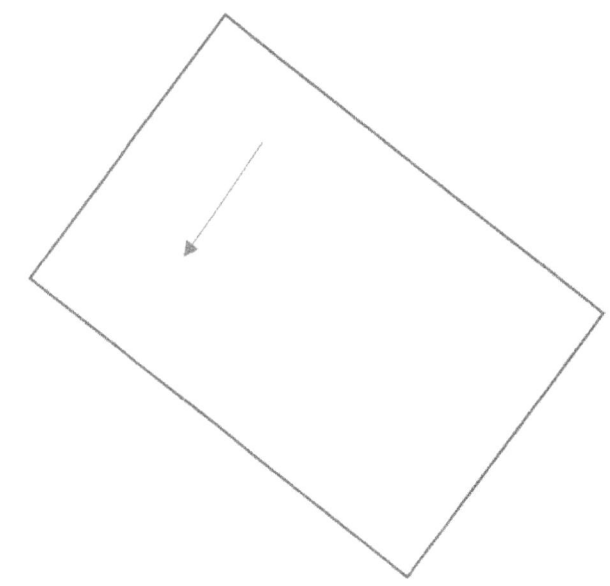

Right-handed people slant their paper to the left.

Hold your pencil like this:
You hold the pencil between the thumb and 2${}^{nd}$ finger (in the bird's beak). The pencil lays against the 3${}^{rd}$ finger. Grip it close to the pencil point for better control. Don't force it. Relax.

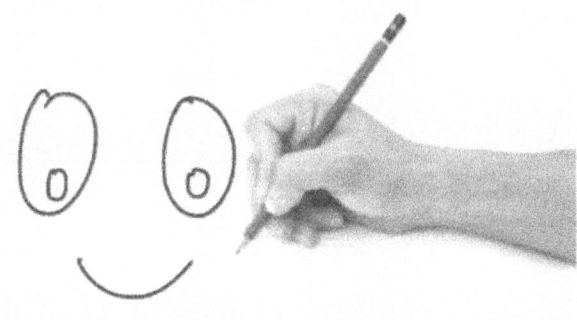

Follow the arrows: Try to make each letter first.

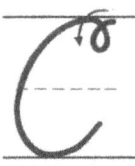 

 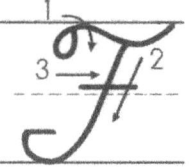

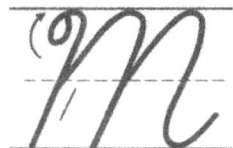 

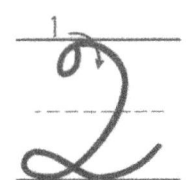 

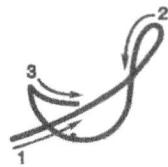
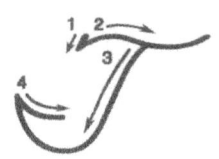

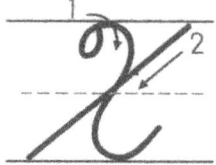
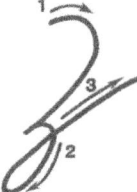

A B C D E F G

H I J K L M N

O P Q R S T U

V W X Y Z

Follow the arrows:   Try to make each letter first.

a   b   c

d   e   f

g   h   i

j   k   l

a b c d e f g

h i j k l m n

o p q r s t u

v w x y z

# Please trace and copy the letters below.    A B C

**Please trace and copy the letters below.    D  E  F**

𝒟 𝒟 𝒟 𝒟 𝒟 𝒟 𝒟 𝒟 𝒟
𝒟 𝒟 𝒟 𝒟 𝒟 𝒟 𝒟 𝒟 𝒟
𝒟 _____

ℰ ℰ ℰ ℰ ℰ ℰ ℰ ℰ ℰ
ℰ ℰ ℰ ℰ ℰ ℰ ℰ ℰ ℰ
ℰ ℰ ℰ _____
ℰ _____

ℱ ℱ ℱ ℱ ℱ ℱ ℱ ℱ ℱ
ℱ ℱ ℱ ℱ ℱ ℱ ℱ ℱ ℱ
ℱ ℱ ℱ ℱ _____
ℱ ℱ _____

# Please trace and copy the letters below.  G  H  I

**Please trace and copy the letters below.    I  J  K**

# Please trace and copy the letters below.   L  M  N

*L L L L L L L L*

*L L L L L L L L*

*L* _____

*L* _____

*m m m m m m m m*

*m m m m m m m m*

*m* _____

*m* _____

*n n n n n n n n*

*n n n n n n n n*

*n* _____

**Please trace and copy the letters below.   O  P  Q  R**

**Please trace and copy the letters below.    R   S   T**

**Please trace and copy the letters below.   U  V  W  X**

# Please trace and copy the letters below.    Y  Z  a

**Please trace and copy the letters below.   b  c  d**

**Please trace and copy the letters below.     e  f  g**

**Please trace and copy the letters below.    h  I  j**

**Please trace and copy the letters below.   j k l m**

*j j* _____

*k k k k k k k k k*
*k k k k k k k k k*
*k k k k k* _____

*k k k* _____

*l l l l l l l l l l*
*l l l l l l l l l l*
*l l* _____

*m m m m   m m m*

**Please trace and copy the letters below.    m  n  o**

**Please trace and copy the letters below.    p   q**

**Please trace and copy the letters below.    r   s   t**

**Please trace and copy the letters below.    u   v   w**

**Please trace and copy the letters below.    x  y  z**

*x x x x x x x x x x*

*x x x* _____

*y y y y y y y y y y*

*y y y y* _____

*y y y* _____

*z z z z z z z z z z*

*z z z z z z z z z z*

*z z z* _____

*z z z* _____

How to link (loop) the letters together

First do it slowly. Take your time. The ends of the letters curl, roll, and reach up and down to touch the next letter already. Some just need a little help from you.

**A b c d**
*Abcd*

**E f g h**
*Efgh*

**I j k l**
*Ijkl*

**M n o p**
*Mnop*

**Q r s t**
*Qrst*

**U v w x**
*Uvwx*

**Y z**
*Yz*

You will get better with practice. Have fun.

Valentine's Day       California

**Jolly rancher**

*Jolly rancher*

**Police car**

*Police car*

*Jolly rancher*  *Police car*

**Abraham Lincoln**

**Goldfish**

*Abraham Lincoln*  *Goldfish*

*Abraham Lincoln Goldfish*

**Motorcycle**

*Motorcycle*

**Eight ball**

*Eight ball*

*Motorcycle*  *Eight ball*

# WIKIPEDIA

**The Free Encyclopedia**
**Wikipedia**

*Wikipedia* (cursive tracing)

Quack quack quack

*Quack quack quack* (cursive tracing)

*Wikipedia   Quack quack quack* (cursive tracing)

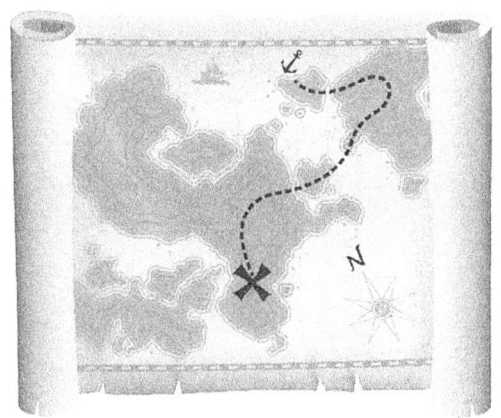
X marks the spot

Volcano

*X marks the spot*   *Volcano*

*X marks the spot   Volcano*

**Football helmet**

*Football helmet*

Kit Kat

*Kit Kat*

*Football helmet       Kit Kat*

Pres. Barack Obama  Dinosaurs

*Pres. Barack Obama   Dinosaurs*

*Pres. Barack Obama   Dinosaurs*

**Happy Hanukkah**

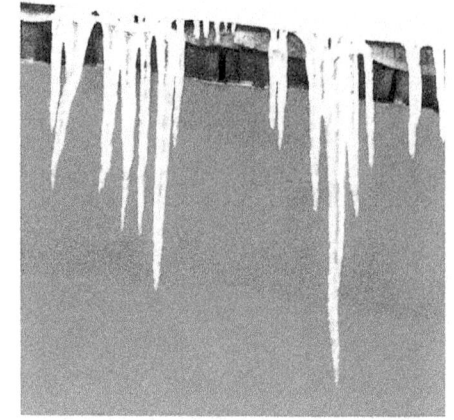

**Icicles**

Campbell's Soup	Grape juice

*Campbell's Soup*	*Grape juice*

*Campbell's Soup Grape juice*

**Statue of Liberty**

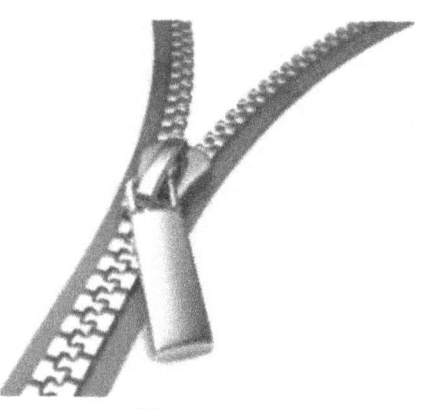
**Zipper**

*Statue of Liberty*     *Zipper*

*Statue of Liberty*     *Zipper*

**Pres. Ronald Reagan**

**Texas**

*Pres. Ronald Reagan*     *Texas*

*Pres. Ronald Reagan*     *Texas*

Ice Breakers

Yawn

United States

Almond Joy

**Frankenstein**

Octopus

*Frankenstein*  *Octopus*

*Frankenstein*  *Octopus*

**George Washington**

**Earth**

*George Washington*　　　*Earth*

*George Washington　　Earth*

**Martin Luther King Jr.**

**Ninjas**

*Martin Luther King Jr.    Ninjas*

*Martin Luther King Jr.    Ninjas*

**Pepperidge Farm**  **Sports car**

*Pepperidge Farm*  *Sports car*

*Pepperidge Farm*  *Sports car*

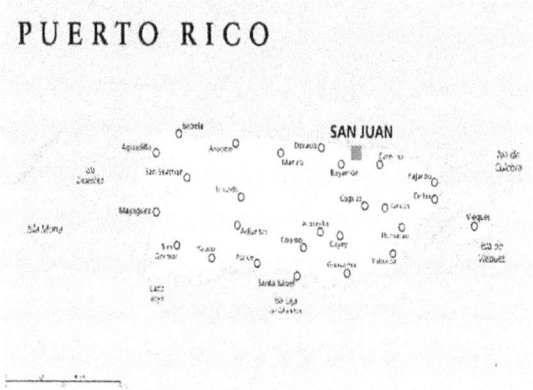

**Puerto Rico**               **Zombie**

*Puerto Rico*                 *Zombie*

*Puerto Rico*                 *Zombie*

**Twizzlers**

*Twizzlers* (cursive tracing)

**Halloween**

*Halloween* (cursive tracing)

*Twizzlers* (cursive tracing)   *Halloween* (cursive tracing)

**Wedding dresses**

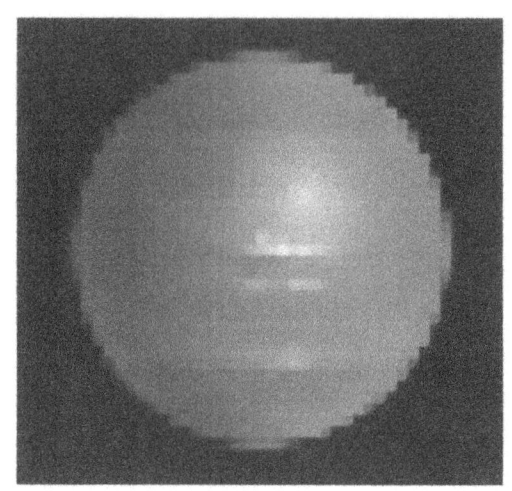

**Neptune**

*Wedding dresses*  *Neptune*

*Wedding dresses*  *Neptune*

**Question mark**

**Spaghetti Os**

**Hardest ones. One more time. Copy across the page.**

*Q*

*q*

*K*

*k*

*F*

*f*

*G*

*Z*

*z*

*Y*

*y*

*s*

## Copy across the page.

B

b

E

H

h

J

j

S

D

I

R

U

**School Words    Copy across the page**

*is*

*it*

*and*

*the*

*of*

*with*

*you*

*your*

*where*

*what*

*when*

*me*

## School Words    Copy across the page

why

how

at

on

be

I

have

has

had

he

her

class

## School Words    Copy across the page

*book*

*Coach*

*period*

*questions*

*Quiz*

*History*

*Gymnasium*

*S A Ts*

*Substitute*

*Hall pass*

*Varsity*

*Main office*

**School Words    Copy across the page**

*Graduation*

*Freshman*

*Sophomore*

*Junior*

*Senior*

*Nurse*

*Honor Roll*

*girlfriend*

*Pep rally*

*boyfriend*

*Auditorium*

*cafeteria*

# How to tell time

## on an

## old-fashioned (Analog)

# Clock

Go through each page slowly,
as many times as you like,
until you "get it."

# The Numbers that you See.

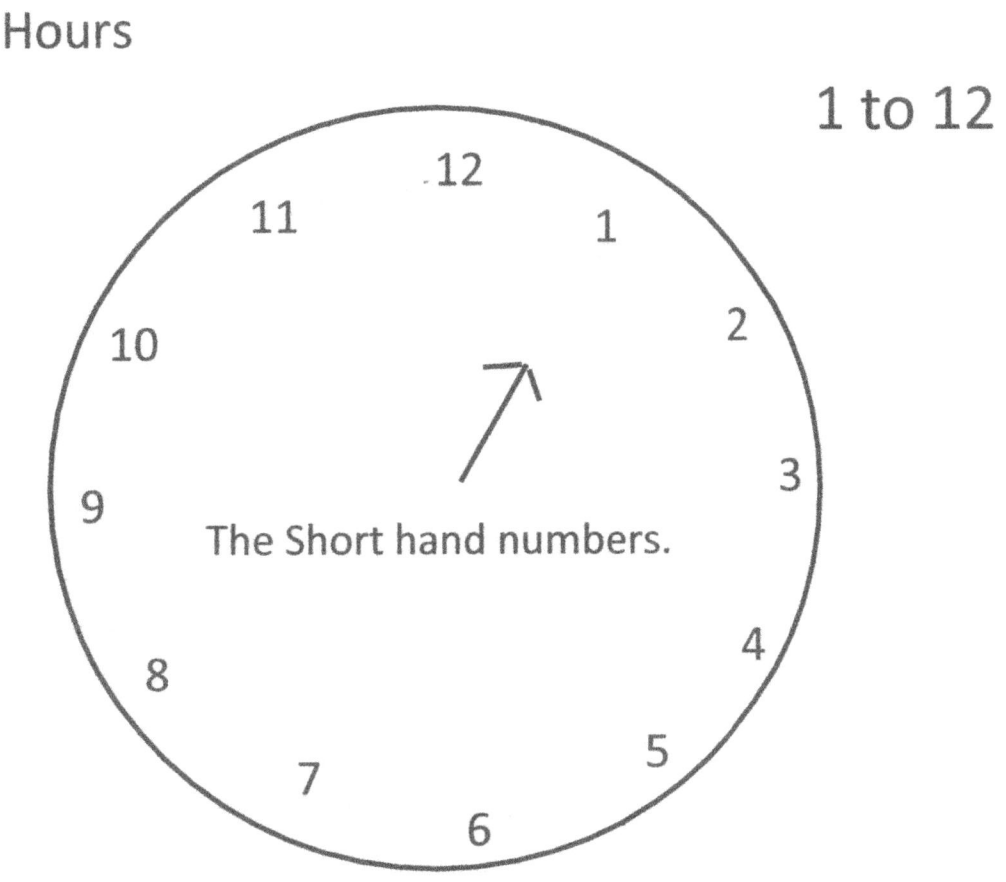

Hours

1 to 12

The Short hand numbers.

These numbers are on every clock or watch. They could be dots, stars or symbols. The Short hand counts the hour numbers—only.

# The Numbers that you Don't see.

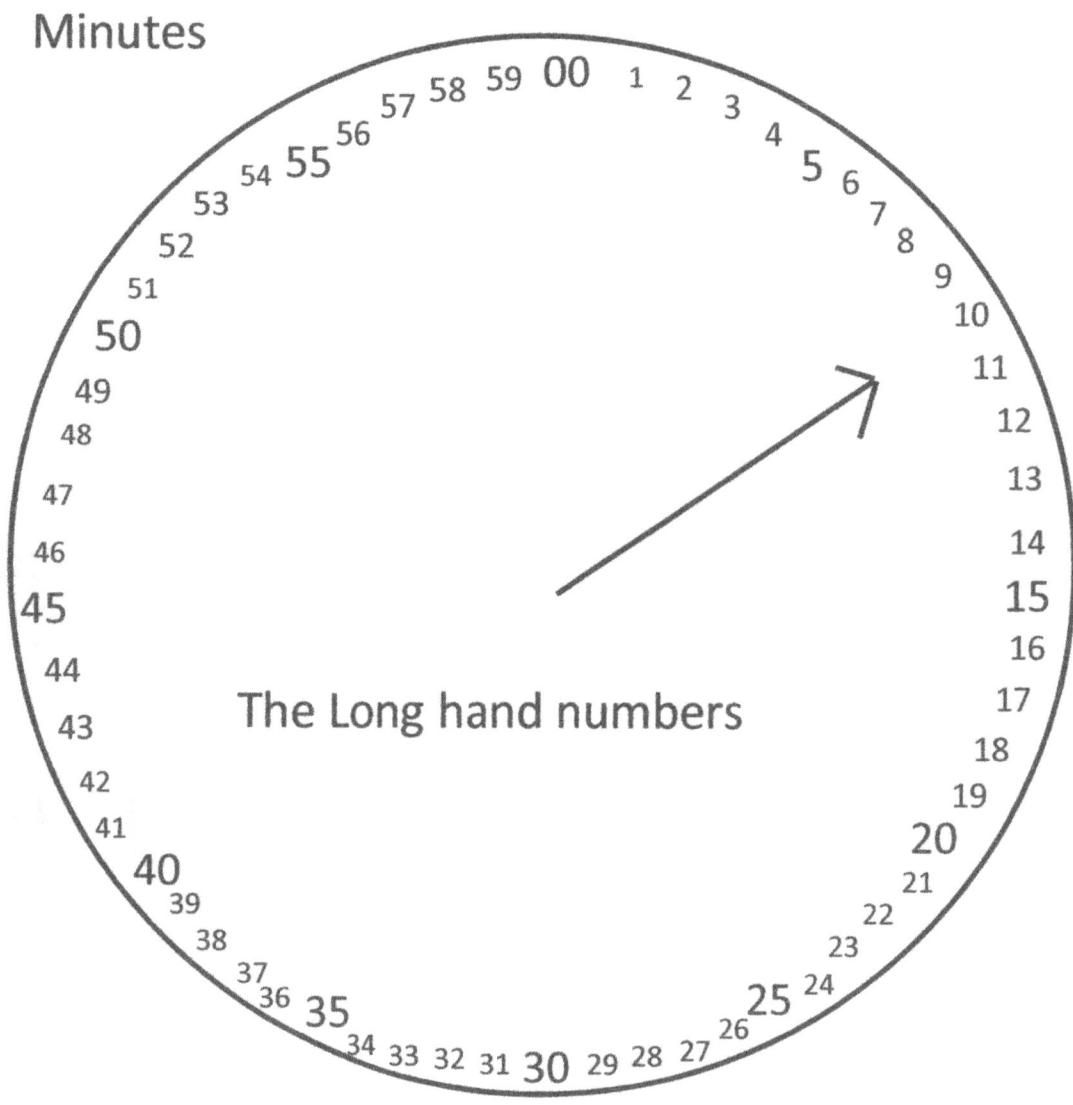

These numbers are on every clock or watch, even if you don't see them. These numbers are called minutes. 1 to 59, 00 = 60. Sixty minutes equals 1 hour. The Long hand counts the minutes—only.

# The Count by 5s

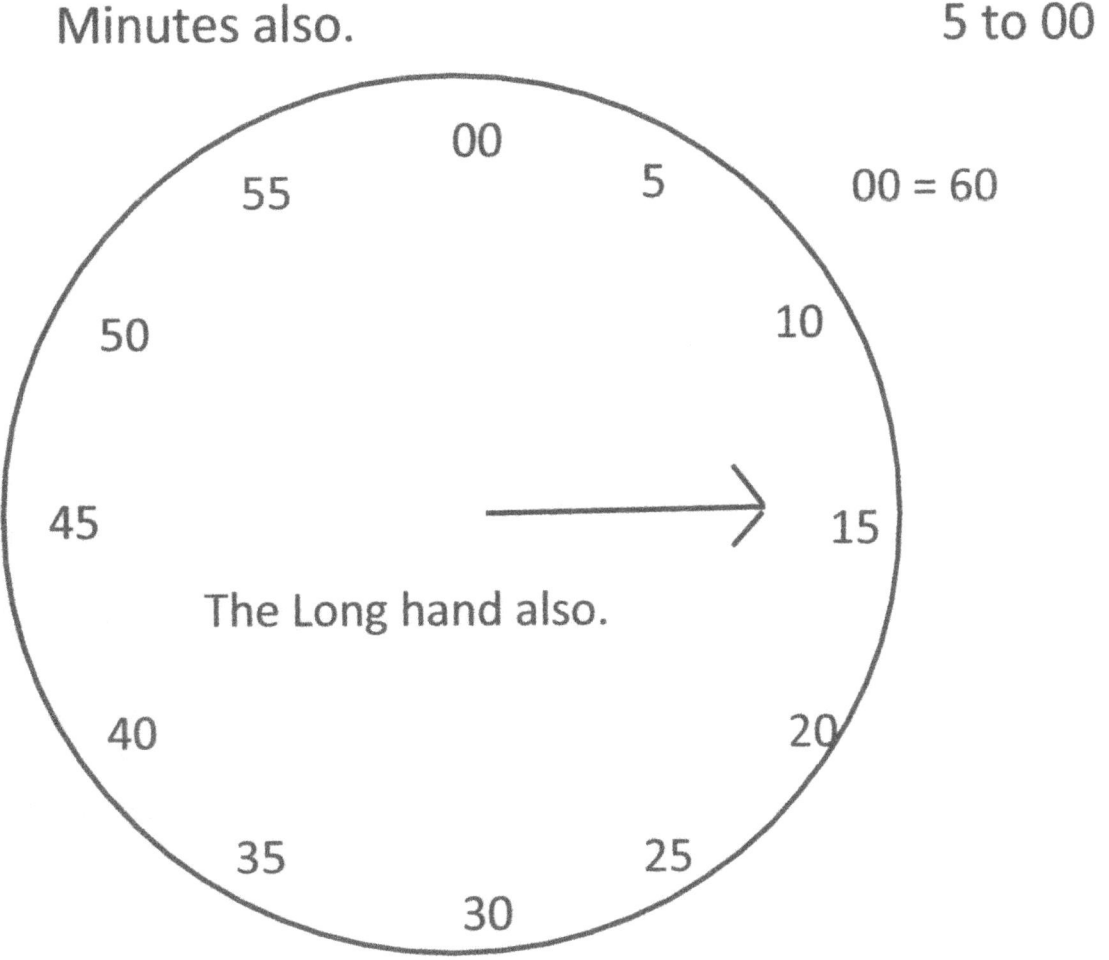

The Count by 5s are on every clock or watch, even if you don't see them. They are part of the Numbers you Don't see. 60 minutes equal 1 hour. The Long hand counts the Count by 5s also.

# Clockwise

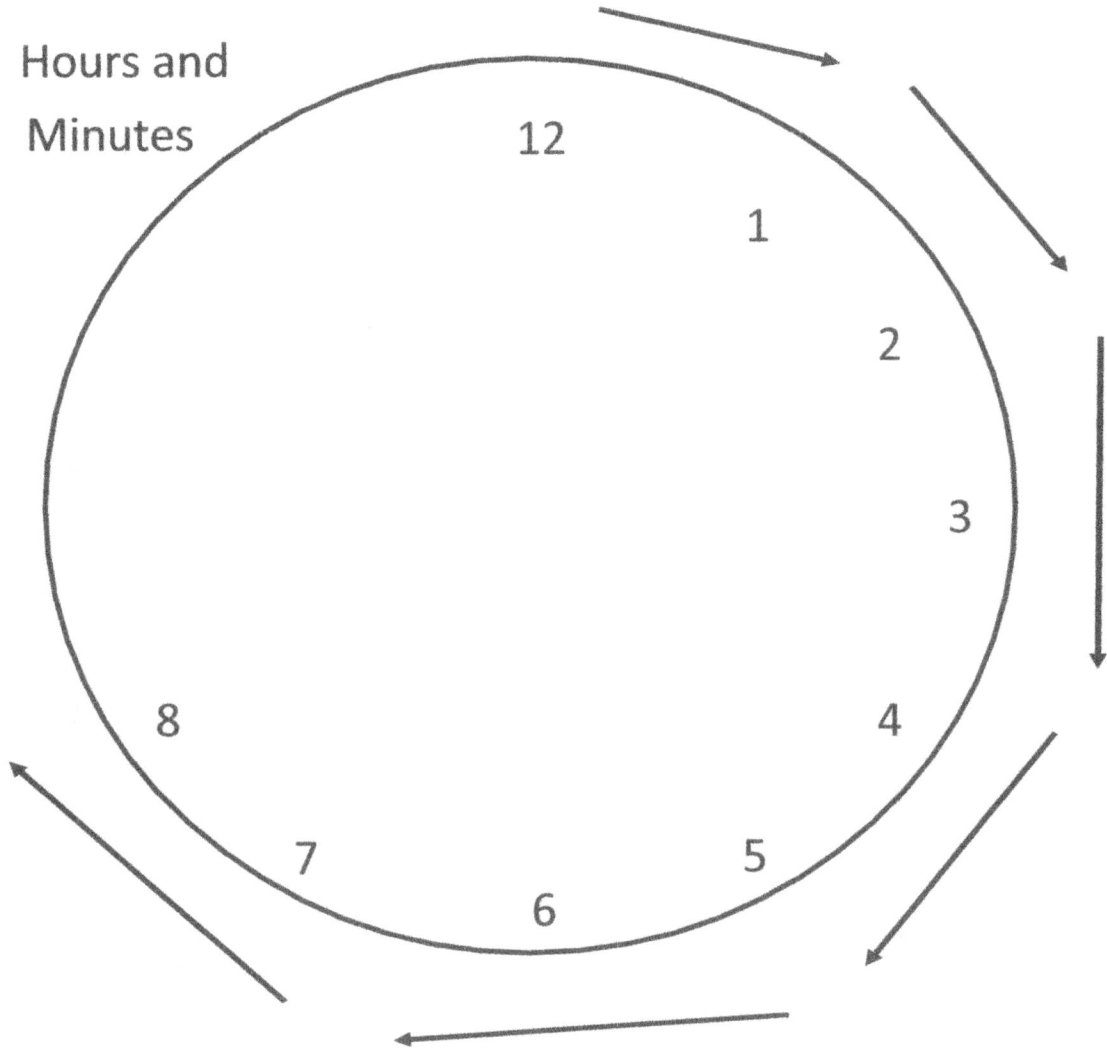

All clocks run clockwise from 1,2,3 to 12 and around and around again. Never the other way! It's just like counting order, never backward. 9 -10 -11-12-1-2-3...

## Dead Center and Hour's Space.

Hours

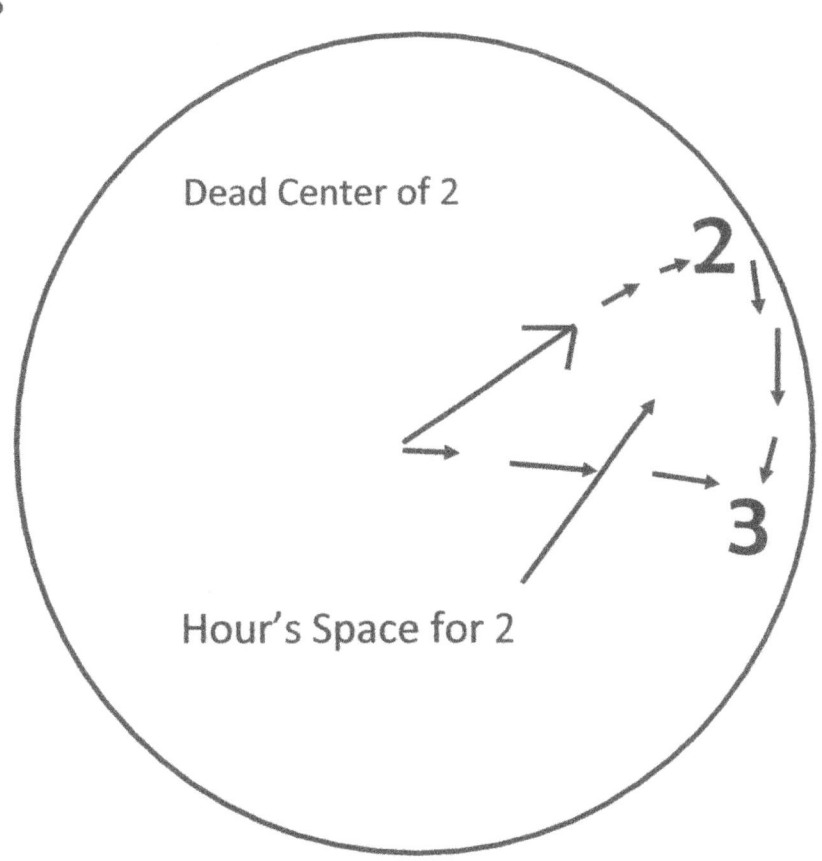

Dead Center is the middle of a number. The hour, all the Space after Dead Center, belongs to that number. In the example above, the short hand is Dead Center on the 2. Everything, after Dead Center belongs to the 2 o'clock hour. 2: 10, 2: 31, 2:43, 2: 55, until Dead Center 3 o'clock. Remember clockwise. It's the same with each number. Dead Center = o'clock or :00

## Dead Center and Hour's Space.

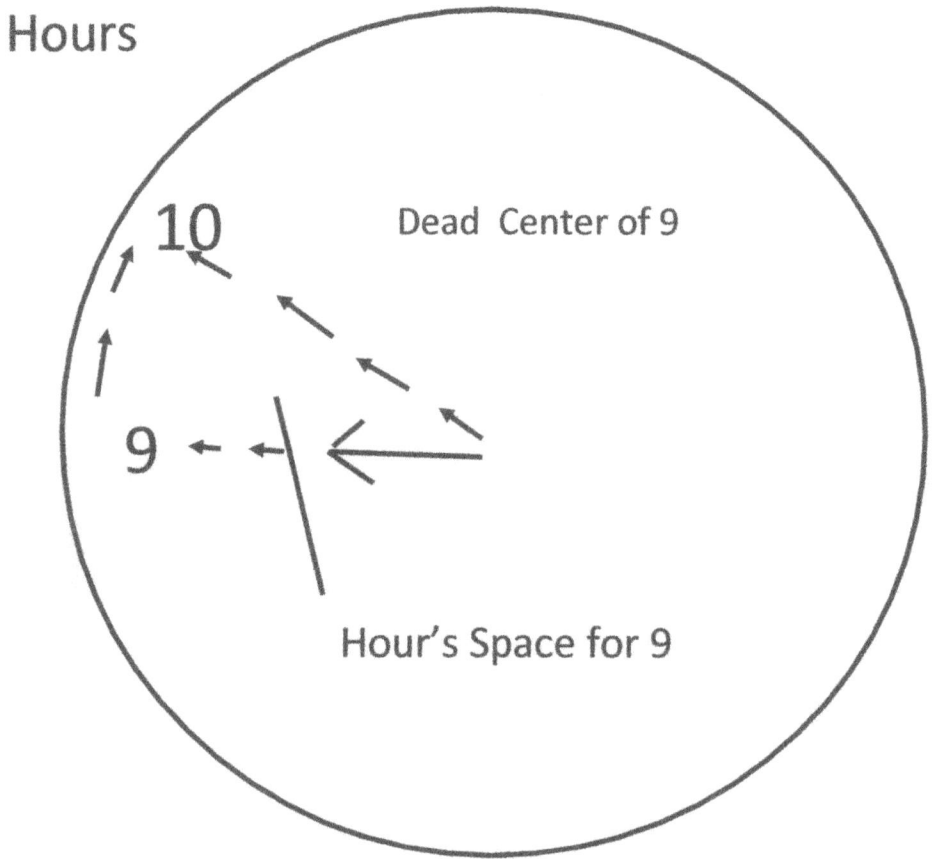

Dead Center is the middle of a number. The hour, all the Space after Dead Center, belongs to that number. In the example above, the short hand is Dead Center on the 9. Everything, after Dead Center belongs to the 9 o'clock hour. 9: 05, 9: 35, 9:42, 9: 58, until Dead Center 10 o'clock. Remember clockwise. It's the same with each number. Dead Center = o'clock or :00

The Numbers that you See. The Numbers you Don't see. The Count by 5s.

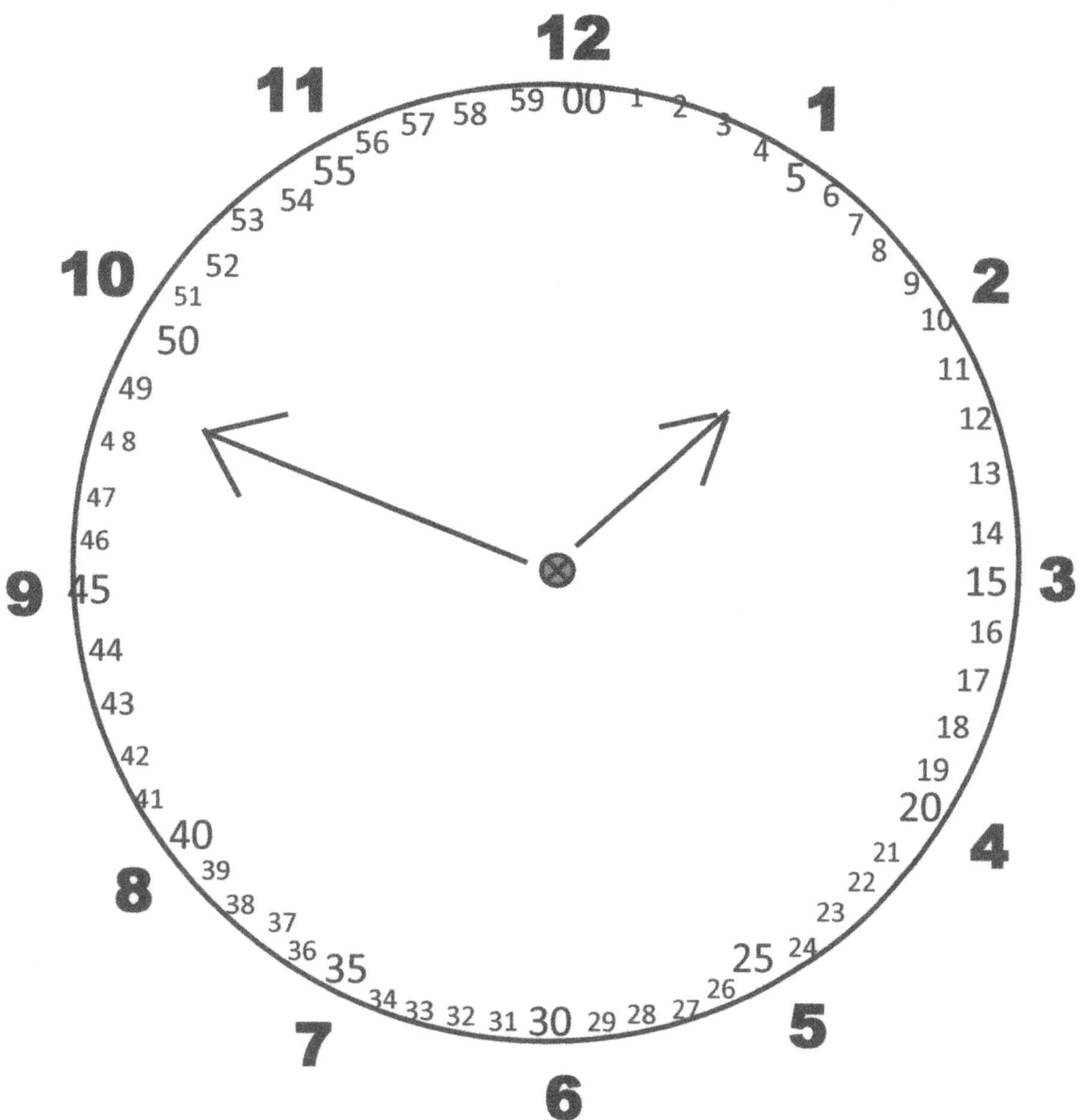

Hours are counted by the short hand only. The hour is 1. Not Dead Center, but the 1 Hour's Space. Minutes are counted by the long hand only. The minute is 49. So, it's 1:49. Looks like it's on the 2, but no! Not yet! Don't be tricked! Eleven more minutes to go before it's 2 o'clock.

The Numbers that you See. The Numbers you Don't see. The Count by 5s.

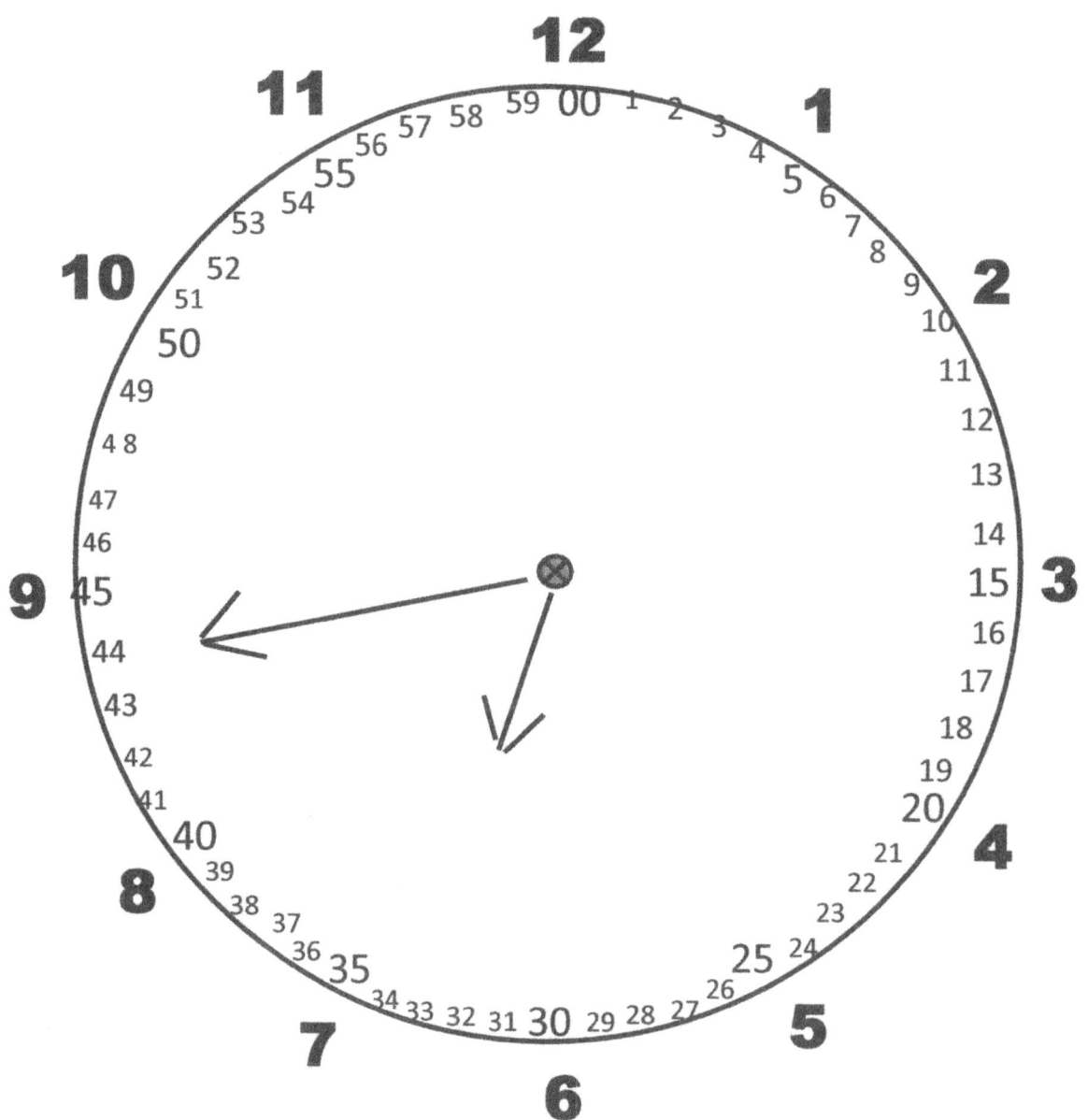

Hours are counted by the short hand only. The hour is 6. Not Dead Center, but the 6 Hour's Space. Minutes are counted by the long hand only. The minute is 44. So, it's 6:44. Looks like it's on the 7, but no! Not yet! Don't be tricked! Sixteen more minutes to go before it's 7 o'clock.

*Take your time, go over the clock pages again. You'll get it. Use your digital clocks to help you. The <u>Numbers that you Don't see</u> are the ones that give people the most trouble. There are so many (1 to 59, 00) that they leave them off clocks. You're just supposed to know there, there.*

*Also remember that...*

*Fifteen minutes is a quarter (1/4<sup>th</sup>) of an hour. As in, a quarter to 5 (4:45) or a quarter after 5 (5:15).*

*Thirty minutes is half an hour. As in, I'll be there in half an hour.*

*It's 2:59 then 3 o'clock, you never say "60".*

*It's 7:59 then 8 o'clock, you never say "60".*

*Sixty seconds equal one minute.*

*Sixty minutes equal one hour.*

*Twenty-four hours equal one whole day.*

*12am is at 12 midnight (past bedtime). 12pm is at 12 noon (lunch time). AM (ante meridiem) means before noon. PM (post meridiem) means after noon.*

## The Pledge of Allegiance     Please copy

*I pledge allegiance to the flag.*

*of the United States of America*

*And to the republic for which it stands*

*one nation under God, indivisible*

*with liberty and justice for all.*

Please copy these great words in cursive. Go on. You know how.

And so, my fellow Americans: ask not what your country can do for you—ask what you can do for your country.

My fellow citizens of the world: ask not what America will do for you, but what together we can do for the freedom of man.

President John F. Kennedy
January 20th, 1961
From his Inaugural address

**Print these great words.   See if you can read them right.**

*"From now on, any definition of a successful life must include serving others."*

President George H. W. Bush [father]
To students at Washington
University about volunteering.
February 18th, 1989

*"Everywhere that freedom stirs, let tyrants fear."*

President George W. Bush [son]
To the sailors on the
USS Abraham Lincoln
on May 1, 2003.

Please copy these great words in cursive.

You can fool some of the people all the time,
and all the people some of the time,
but you can't fool all the people all the time.

                                      President Abraham Lincoln

## Don't stop!   You're on a roll!!!

Keep practicing. Get another workbook when your done with this one. Use your new cursive hand every chance you get.

When reading, pick a word, any word, and write it over and over. Practice during free time, like when your alone in your room.

Use it a little bit each day until you're confident that your handwriting is as good as anyone else's.

Ms. Murphy,
I mean, Jonell

"Hey! We have a Sub!!!"

Milton Keynes UK
Ingram Content Group UK Ltd.
UKHW030249090923
428338UK00004B/49